16 . … ENTS +
… ACKING TRACKS +
16 mp… … MO TRACKS!*

PLAYALONG PIANO 16 CHART HITS!

WISE PUBLICATIONS
part of The Music Sales Group
London / New York / Paris / Sydney / Copenhagen / Berlin / Madrid / Hong Kong / Tokyo

Published by
WISE PUBLICATIONS
14-15 Berners Street, London W1T 3LJ,
United Kingdom.

Exclusive Distributors:
MUSIC SALES LIMITED
Distribution Centre, Newmarket Road, Bury St Edmunds, Suffolk IP33 3YB,
United Kingdom.
MUSIC SALES PTY LIMITED
Units 3-4, 17 Willfox Street, Condell Park, NSW 2200, Australia.

Order No. AM1009492
ISBN 978-1-78305-725-2

Compiled and edited by Jenni Norey.
Backing tracks by Paul Honey and Christopher Hussey.
Cover/prelims designed by Michael Bell Design.
Printed in the EU.

www.musicsales.com

BEST THING I NEVER HAD
(Edmonds/Dixon/Smith/Knowles/Griffin/McCampbell/Taylor)
EMI Music Publishing Limited/Edward Kassner Music Company Limited/
Universal/MCA Music Limited/Warner/Chappell North America Limited/
Bug Music (Windswept Account)/Keys In Motion Publishing

HOW LONG WILL I LOVE YOU
(Scott)
Sony/ATV Music Publishing (UK) Limited

I NEED A DOLLAR
(Michels/Blacc/Movshon/Silverman)
Universal Music Publishing Limited/EMI Music Publishing Limited/
Kobalt Music Publishing Limited

JUST GIVE ME A REASON
(Levine/Mars/Lawrence/Cain/Walton)
Bug Music Limited/Warner/Chappell North America Limited/Universal/
MCA Music Limited/Bug Music (Windswept Account)

JUST THE WAY YOU ARE
(Levine/Mars/Lawrence/Cain/Walton)
Bug Music Limited/Warner/Chappell North America Limited/Universal/
MCA Music Limited/Bug Music (Windswept Account)

LET GO FOR TONIGHT
(Hull/Allen)
Universal Music Publishing Limited/BMG Rights Management (UK) Limited

LET IT GO
(Lopez/Anderson-Lopez)
Warner/Chappell Artemis Music Limited

NEXT TO ME
(Craze/Chegwin/Sande/Paul)
EMI Music Publishing Limited/Sony/ATV Music Publishing (UK) Limited/
BMG Rights Management (UK) Limited

A NIGHT LIKE THIS
(Schreurs/Degiorgio/Wieringen)
Collect Music Publishers BV/Eagle-I Music Limited/
Grandmono Music Publishing

SAY SOMETHING
(Campbell/Vaccarino/Axel)
Universal/MCA Music Limited/ST Music LLC

A SKY FULL OF STARS
(Berryman/Buckland/Champion/Martin/Bergling)
Universal Music Publishing MGB Limited/EMI Music Publishing Limited

SOMEWHERE ONLY WE KNOW
(Hughes/Rice-Oxley/Chaplin)
Universal Music Publishing MGB Limited

SPEECHLESS
(Germanotta)
Sony/ATV Music Publishing (UK) Limited

STAY WITH ME
(Smith/Napier/Phillips)
Universal Music Publishing Limited/Sony/ATV Music Publishing (UK) Limited

A THOUSAND YEARS
(Hodges/Perri)
EMI Music Publishing Limited/Warner/Chappell North America Limited/
Fintage Publishing B.V.

TURNING TABLES
(Tedder/Adkins)Universal Music Publishing Limited/
Kobalt Music Publishing Limited

Best Thing I Never Had

Words & Music by Kenneth Edmonds, Antonio Dixon, Patrick Smith, Beyoncé Knowles,
Larry Griffin, Caleb McCampbell & Robert Taylor

B F♯ D♯m C♯ B F♯
a time I thought that you did
(2.) you're hurt. Boo hoo. Oh, did you ex-
D♯m C♯ B F♯ D♯m C♯
ev - 'ry - thing right. No lies, no wrong. Boy, I
-pect me to care? You don't de - serve my tears.
B F♯ D♯m C♯
must have been out of my mind. So when I
I guess that's why they ain't there. When I think that
G♯m7 D♯m7 C♯ G♯m7
think of the time that I al - most loved you,
there was a time that I al - most loved you,
you showed your ass and I,

Bm(maj7)
G♯m
F♯/A♯
I saw the re-al you. Thank God you blew it, thank God I dodged the bul-let. I'm so
B
C♯sus4
o-ver you, so ba-by good look-in' out. I want-ed you bad.
F♯
B
D♯m
C♯
I'm so through with it. 'Cause hon-est-ly you turned out to be the...
You turned out to be the... And I'm
(Best thing I nev-er had.) (Best thing I nev-er had.)

F♯ B D♯m C♯ Bmaj9
To Coda
gon' al-ways be the...
(Best thing you nev - er had.)
I bet it
1. C♯
2. C♯
sucks to be you right now.
2. So sad.
D♯m Bm/D
I know you want me back.
It's times to face the facts, that
8va
C♯ G♯/B♯
I'm the one that's got a - way.
Lord knows that it would take an - oth - er

Badd9
F♯/A♯
place, an-oth-er time, an-oth-er world, an-oth-er life. Thank
G♯m7
F♯/A♯
Badd9
D.S. al Coda
God I found the good in good-bye. I used to want you so bad.
Coda
Bmaj9
Best thing you nev - er had. I used to want you so bad.
F♯
B
D♯m
C♯
I'm so through with that. 'Cause hon - est - ly you

F♯ B D♯m C♯ F♯ B
turned out to be the... You turned out to be the...
(Best thing I nev - er had.)
D♯m C♯ F♯ B D♯m C♯
And I will nev-er be the...
(Best thing I nev - er had.) (Best thing you nev - er had.)
Bmaj9 C♯
Oh, ba-by, I bet it sucks to be you right now.

F♯
B
D♯m
C♯/E♯
F♯
B
(Goes a - round, comes back a - round.)
(Goes a - round, comes back a - round.)
Bet it
D♯m
C♯
F♯
B
D♯m
C♯/E♯
(Goes a - round comes back a - round.)
sucks to be you right now.
Bet it sucks to be you right now.
rit.
F♯
B
D♯m
C♯
F♯
(Goes a - round comes back a - round.)
Bet it sucks to be you right now.

How Long Will I Love You

Words & Music by Mike Scott

F C Dm C(sus4) C(sus2) G
As long as the sea-sons need_ to fol-low their plan.
As long as your fa - ther told_ you, as long_ as you can.
F F(sus2) Dm G/B C
How long will I be with you? As long as the sea is bound_ to_
How long will I give_ to you? As long as I_ live through you
F Dm G
wash up - on the sand.
how-ev - er long you say.
C G F C
How long will I love_ you?_ As long as stars are a - bove you

Dm C(sus4) C(sus2) G
and lon - ger if I may.
C G F C Dm C(sus4) C G
Mm. Mm, mm.
slow
C G/B Am(add9) G G9(omit5)/F G(add9) C
How long will I love you? As long as stars are a-bove you.

I Need A Dollar

Words & Music by Leon Michels, Aloe Blacc,
Nicholas Movshon & Jeffrey Silverman

Dbm Abm Gb
dol-lar is what I need, and if I share with you my stor-y, would you
1° only
Dbm Ebm Abm Gb
share your dol-lar with me? Bad times are com-in' and I
Dbm Abm Gb
reap what I don't sow. (Hey hey.) Well, let me tell you some-thin',
Dbm Abm Gb
all that glit-ters ain't gold. (Hey hey.) It's been a long old troub-le,

D♭m A♭m G♭
long old troub-le-some road, and I'm look-in' for some-bod-y, come and
D♭m E♭m A♭m G♭
help me car-ry this load. I need a dol-lar, dol-lar,
D♭m A♭m G♭
dol-lar is what I need. (Hey hey.) Well, I need dol-lar, dol-lar,
straight 16s
D♭m E♭m E♭m7 A♭m
dol-lar is what I need. Well, I don't know if I'm

D♭m
E♭m7
A♭m
walk - in' on sol - id ground,
'cause ev - 'ry - thing a - round me
D♭m
E♭m7
A♭m
is fall - in' down.
2º crumbl - in'
And all I want is for some -
D♭m
E♭m
one to help me.
1.
swung 16s
A♭m
G♭
D♭m
I had a job, but the boss man let me go.
(He said:)
4fr
6fr

A♭m G♭ D♭m
"I'm sor - ry, but I won't be need - in' your help no more." (I said:)
A♭m G♭ D♭m
"Please, mis - ter boss man, I need this job more than you know." But he
A♭m G♭ D♭m E♭m
gave me my last pay - check and he sent me on out the door.
2.
straight 16s
E♭m7 D♭m7 E♭m7 D♭m7
What in the world am I gon - na do to - mor - row?

E♭m7
6fr
D♭m7
4fr
E♭m7
6fr
D♭m7
5fr
Is there some-one with a dol-lar I could bor-row?
3
3
Who can help me take a-way my sor-row?
swung 16s
N.C.
E♭m
6fr
May-be it's in-side the bot-tle, may-be it's in-side the bot-tle...
A♭m
4fr
G♭
D♭m
4fr
I had some good old bud-dies, names is whis-key and wine. (Hey hey.)
Your mam-ma may have blessed the child that's got his own. (Hey hey.)

A♭m
G♭
D♭m
4fr
And for my good old bud-dies, I spent my last dime. (Hey hey.)
If God has plans for me, I hope it ain't writ in stone. (Hey hey.)
Now wine is good to me, it help me pass the time, and my
Be-cause I've been work-in', work-in' my-self down to the bone, and I
E♭m
6fr
good old bud-dy, whis-key, keep me warm-er than sun-shine. (Hey hey.)
swear on grand-pa's grave, I'll be paid when I come home. (Hey hey.)

A♭m
G♭
D♭m
Well, I need dol-lar, dol-lar, dol-lar is what I need. (Hey hey.)
A♭m
G♭
D♭m
Said I need dol-lar, dol-lar, dol-lar that what I need. (Hey hey.)
A♭m
G♭
D♭m
Well, I need dol-lar, dol-lar, dol-lar that what I need, and if I
A♭m
G♭
D♭m
E♭m
share with you my stor-y, would you share your dol-lar with me? Come on,

Abm
Gb
Dbm
4fr
share your dol-lar with me, go 'head, share your dol-lar with me. Come on,
Abm
Gb
Dbm
share your dol-lar, gim-me your dol-lar, share your dol-lar with me, come on,
Abm
Gb
Dbm
share your dol-lar with me.
Abm
Gb
Dbm
Ebm
Abm
6fr

Just Give Me A Reason

Words & Music by Alecia Moore, Jeff Bhasker
& Nate Ruess

C G Em D A/C♯
ev - 'ry touch you fixed them. Now you've been talk - ing in your
D Em D A/C♯ D
sleep, oh, oh, things you nev - er say to me, oh, oh.
Em D A/C♯ D G/B C G/B Dsus4 D
Tell me that you've had e - nough of our love, our love.
G D/F♯ Em Bm
Just give me a rea - son, just a lit - tle bit's e - nough, just a se - cond we're not bro - ken just bent

D7 G D/F#
and we can learn to love a-gain. It's in the stars, it's been writ-ten in the scars on our hearts.
Em Bm D7 G
We're not bro-ken just bent and we can learn to love a-gain. I'm
C Em C
sor-ry I don't un-der-stand where all of this is com-ing from, I thought that we were fine.
G C Em
Your head is run-ning wild a-gain, my dear we still have ev-'ry-thing and
(Oh, we had ev-'ry-thing.)

C G Em D A/C♯ D
it's all_ in_ your mind.__ (Yeah but this is hap-pen-ing.) You've been hav- in' real bad_ dreams, oh, oh, you
Em D A/C♯ D Em D A/C♯ D G/B
used to lie so close to__ me, oh, oh. There's noth-ing more than emp - ty__ sheets be-tween our_
C G/B Am C G/B Dsus4 D
love, our love, oh our love, our love. Oh,
G D/F♯ Em Bm
just give me a rea-son, just a lit - tle bit's e-nough, just a se-cond we're not bro-ken just bent_

D7
G
D/F♯
and we can learn to love a-gain.
I nev-er stopped, you're still writ-ten in the scars on my heart.
Em
Bm
D7
Em
You're not bro-ken just bent and we can learn to love a-gain.
Oh tear ducts and rust,
Bm
C
D
I'll fix it for us,
we're col-lec-ting dust but our love's e-nough.
Em
Bm
C
You're hold-ing it in,
you're pour-ing a drink,
no noth-ing is as

Am
D
N.C.
bad as it seems, we'll come clean. Just give me a rea-son, just a
lit-tle bit's e-nough, just a se-cond we're not bro-ken just bent and we can learn to love a-gain.
It's in the stars, it's been writ-ten in the scars on our hearts that we're not bro-ken just bent
and we can learn to love a-gain. Just give me a rea-son, just a lit-tle bit's e-nough, just a
G
D/F♯

Em Bm D7 G
se-cond we're not bro-ken just bent and we can learn to love a-gain. It's in the stars, it's been
D/F♯ Em Bm D7
writ-ten in the scars on our hearts that we're not bro-ken just bent and we can learn to love a-gain.
G D/F♯ Em Bm D7
(We can learn to love a-gain.)
(We can learn to love a-gain.)
Em D A/C♯ D G/B C G/B Am G

Just The Way You Are

Words & Music by Ari Levine, Bruno Mars,
Philip Lawrence, Khari Cain & Khalil Walton

F/B♭
per - fect - ly___ with - out her try - ing.
She's so beau - ti - ful___
F
and I tell her ev - 'ry___ day.___
Yeah,_
I know, I know___ when I com - pli - ment___ her she won't be - lieve me.
Dm
And it's so, it's so___ sad to think that she___ don't see___ what I see.

F/B♭
But ev-'ry time she asks me "Do I look o-kay?" I say:
F
When I see your face,
F
Dm7
there's not a thing that I would change 'cause you're a-maz-
F/B♭
-ing just the way you are.
F

And when you smile,
the whole world stops
Dm7
F/B♭
and stares for a while.
'Cause girl you're a - maz - ing
just
F
the way you are.
Yeah.
2. Her lips, her lips I could kiss them all day if she'd let me.

Dm7
Her laugh, her laugh, she hates, but I think it's so sex - y.
F/B♭
She's so beau - ti - ful and I tell her ev - 'ry
F
day. Oh you know, you know, you know I'd nev - er
Dm7
ask you to change. If per-fect's what you're search-ing for then just stay the same. So

F/B♭
don't e-ven both-er ask-ing if you look o-kay, you know I'll
F
say:
When I see your
F
face,
there's not a
Dm7
thing that I would change 'cause you're a-maz-
F/B♭
-ing just the way you
F
are.

And when you smile,
the whole world stops
Dm7
F/B♭
and stares for a while.
'Cause girl, you're a - maz - ing
just
F
the way you are.
The way you are,
Dm7
the way you are,

F/B♭
girl, you're a - maz - ing just the way you are.
F
When I see your face,
Dm7
there's not a thing that I would change
F/B♭
'cause you're a - maz - ing just

F
the way you are.
And when you smile,
Dm7
the whole world stops and stares for a while.
F/B♭
'Cause girl, you're a - maz - ing just
F
the way you are.
Yeah.

Let Go For Tonight

Words & Music by Thomas Hull & Louisa Allen

Fmaj7
G
Am
- ing, leav-ing our foot - prints on the ground.
(8)
Fmaj7
G
Am
It might be a prayer or may-be a piece
(2.) I wan-na drive. I wan-na drive
8vb
Em7
Fmaj7
G
of con - ver-sa - tion. Wher-ev-er we go we make a sound.
in - to the o - pen, look-in' for rea - sons I can't find.
(8)
Am
F(add9)
So I call your name, the on-ly
(8)

G
Em
Am
F(add9)
thing I know is I need you here or you'll be gone for-ev-er. All that I know, all
(8)
G
Em
F
that I know is we're here to - night. * Turn off the lights.
(8)
Am
G
Em7
Let go for to-night ba - by. Let love in your life
Fmaj7
Am
G
and be strong. Let go for to-night ba - by.

Em7 Fmaj7 Am G
Who needs sleep to - night. I need to let go, let it go.
Em7 Fmaj7 Am G
Let go, let it go. Turn off the lights. Let love in your life ba - by.
1. 2, 3.
Em7 Fmaj7 Fmaj7
Who needs sleep to - night. I need to
F C Am Em
let go, let it go. Let go, let it go. I need to
8vb

F C G
To Coda
let go, let it go before we're gone, gone, gone.
(8)
Fmaj7 G
So I call your name, the on - ly thing I know is I need
(cue)
(8)
Em7 F Fmaj7
you here or you'll be gone for - ev - er. All that I know, all
G Em F
that I know is I need you here or you'll be gone for - ev - er.

Fmaj9 G Em7 Am
Turn off the lights.
8va
8vb
Fmaj7 G Em7 F
D.S. al Coda
Turn of the lights.
(8)
Coda
G Fmaj7 G7 Am
8vb to end
Fell from the sky. We fell from the sky
(cue)
8vb
Em7 Fmaj7 G7 Am
and start - ed walk - ing, leav - ing our foot - prints on the ground.

Let It Go

Words & Music by Robert Lopez & Kristen Anderson-Lopez

Fm Db Eb Bb(sus4) Bb
king-dom of i - so-la - tion, and it looks like I'm the Queen.
Fm Db Eb Bb(sus4) Bbm
The wind is howl - ing like this swirl - ing storm in - side,
Fm Eb Bb
could-n't keep it in, heav-en knows I tried.
Eb Db
Don't let them in, don't let them see, be the good girl you al-ways have to be,
4fr
6fr

E♭
D♭
6fr
4fr
— con-ceal, — don't feel, — don't let — them know, — well, now —
A♭
E♭
— they know. — Let it go, — let it go, — can't —
Fm
D♭
A♭
E♭
hold it back an-y - more. Let it go, — let it go, — turn a-way —
Fm
D♭
A♭
E♭
— and slam — the — door. — I — don't — care — what they're

Fm
D♭
4fr
Cm
3fr
B
go - ing to say, let the storm rage on, the
D♭
4fr
A♭
4fr
E♭/G
cold nev - er both - ered me an - y - way.
Fm
D♭
4fr
E♭
6fr
B♭m
2. It's fun - ny how some dis - tance makes ev - 'ry - thing seem small and the
Fm
E♭
6fr
B♭(sus4)
B♭
fears that once con - trolled me can't get to me at all.

E♭
D♭
It's time to see what I can do, to test the li - mits and break through,
E♭
D♭
no right, no wrong, no rules for me. I'm free.
N.C.
A♭
E♭
Let it go, let it go, I am one
Fm
D♭
A♭
E♭
with the wind and sky. Let it go, let it go, you'll nev-

Fm
D♭
4fr
A♭
4fr
E♭
6fr
- er see me cry.
Here I stand and
Fm
D♭
4fr
Cm
3fr
B
here I'll stay, let the storm rage on.
D♭
4fr
My pow - er flur - ries through the air in - to the ground,

my soul is spi - ral - ing in fro - zen frac - tals all a - round
Eb
6fr
and one thought cry - stal - li - zes like an i - cy blast,
Fm
Db
4fr
Eb
6fr
Bbm
I'm nev - er go - ing back, the past is in the past.
Db
4fr
N.C.
Ab
4fr
Eb
6fr
Let it go, let it go and I'll rise

Fm
D♭
A♭
E♭
like the break of dawn. Let it go, let it go, that per-
Fm
D♭
A♭
E♭
-fect girl is gone. Here I stand in the
Fm
D♭
D♭m
Cm
B
light of day, let the storm rage on,
D♭(add9)
the cold nev-er both-ered me an-y-way.

Next To Me

Words & Music by Harry Craze, Hugo Chegwin,
Emeli Sandé & Anup Kumar Paul

Am
G/B
C
You won't ev - er find him be- un- faith - ful.
You will find
You won't ev - er find him where the rest go.
You will find
Am
G/B
C
1.
2.
C
him, you'll find him next to me.
him, you'll find him next to me.
Next to me,
Am
G/B
C
Am
G/B
ooh.
Next to me,
ooh.
C
Am
G/B
Next to me,
ooh.

C
Am
G/B
C
You will find him, you'll find him next to me.
3.When the
Am
G/B
C
mon-ey's spent and all my friends have van - ished and I can't
(4.) skies are grey and all the doors are clos - ing and the
2° only
Am
G/B
C
seem to find no help or love for free.
ris - ing pres - sure makes it hard to breathe. When all I
Am
G/B
C
I know there's no need for me to pan - ic. 'Cause I'll find
need's a hand to stop the tears from fall - ing. I will find

1.
2.
Am G/B C
him, I'll find him next to me. 4. When the
him, I'll find him next to me.
C Am G/B C
Next to me, ooh. Next to me,
Am G/B C Am G/B
ooh. Next to me, ooh.
C Am G C
I will find him, I'll find him next to me. When the

Fmaj7
G7/B
C
end has come and build - ings fall - ing down fast, when we
Fmaj7
G7/B
Am7
Fmaj7
G/B
spoilt the land and dried up all the sea.
When ev-'ry-one has lost their heads a-round
C
Am
G7/B
C
us. You will find him, you'll find him next to me.
Next to me,
Am
G/B
C
Am
G/B
ooh.
Next to me,
ooh.

1.
C
Am
G/B
C
Next to me, ooh. You will find
Am
G/B
C
him, you'll find him next to me. Next to me,
2.
Fmaj7
G/B
C
ooh. You will find
Am
G/B
C
N.C.
him, you'll find him next to me.

A Night Like This

Words by David Schreurs, Vincent Degiorgio & Jan Van Wieringen
Music by David Schreurs & Vincent Degiorgio

G♯7
4fr
cards. And you walk o - ver, soft - ly mov - ing past the guards. The
chimes? To hear that some - one de - bon - naire has just ar - rived and
C♯m6
stakes are get - ting high - er you can feel it in your heart. He calls your
o - pened up to see my world be - fore my eyes? That sil - hou -
bluff. He is the ace. You nev - er thought he'd played that
- ette cre - ates an im - age on the night I can't for -
G♯7
4fr
much. And now it's more than all his cards you want to touch. You
- get. It has the scent of some - thing spe - cial. I can't rest; if
3

C♯m6
nev-er know if win-ning this could real - ly be e-nough. Take a
I re - sist temp-ta-tion, oh, I know for sure that I will lose the bet.
F♯m6/A
G♯7
4fr
C♯m6
look be-yond the moon, you'll see the stars.
Walk a-way and sud-den-ly it seems I'm not a - lone.
F♯m6/A
G♯7
4fr
And when you look a-round you know the room by
In front of me he stands, I stop be-fore he
C♯
4fr
N.C.
heart.
goes.
D♯m7(add11)
6fr
I have nev-er dreamed it. Have you ev-er

G♯7
C♯6
dreamed a night_ like this?___
I can-not be-
D♯m7(add11)
G♯7
C♯6
-lieve it. I may nev-er see a night_ like this.___
D♯m7(add11)
G♯7
When ev-'ry-thing you think is in - com-plete___ starts hap-pen-ing when
C♯6
F♯m6/A
you are cheek to cheek. Could you ev-er dream it? I have nev-er

1.
G♯7
C♯m6
To Coda
dreamed, dreamed a night like this.
2.
C♯m6
2. How man-y
this.
(guitar solo)
G♯7
C♯m6

Em6
D♯m6
Dm6
Ooh, ooh, ooh, ooh,
C♯m6
Em6
ooh.
Ooh, ooh,
D♯m6
Dm6
C♯6
4fr
D.S. al Coda
ooh, ooh, ooh.
I have nev-er
Coda C♯m6
C♯m9(maj7)
this.

A Sky Full Of Stars

Words & Music by Guy Berryman, Jonathan Buckland,
William Champion, Christopher Martin & Tim Bergling

A♯m7
D♯m7
C♯7(sus4)
F♯/B
6fr
4fr
I'm gon - na give you my heart.
I wan - na die in your arms.
F♯
A♯m7
D♯m7
C♯7(sus4)
'Cause you're a
'Cause you get
F♯/B
F♯
A♯m7
sky, 'cause you're a sky full of stars.
light - er the more it gets dark.
D♯m7
C♯7(sus4)
F♯/B
F♯
'Cause you light up the path.
I'm gon - na give you my heart.

A♯m7
D♯m7
C♯7(sus4)
B
And I don't care, go on and
F♯
A♯m7
D♯m7
C♯7(sus4)
tear me a - part.
And I don't care
B
F♯
A♯m7
if you do.
Ooh.
Ooh.
D♯m7
C♯7(sus4)
B
F♯
'Cause in a sky, 'cause in a sky full of stars
6fr
4fr

A♯m7
D♯m7
C♯7(sus4)
6fr
4fr
I think I saw you.
2º see
B
To Coda
F♯
A♯m7
D♯m7
C♯7(sus4)
B
F♯
A♯m7/E♯
D♯m7
C♯7(sus4)
B

F♯
A♯m7/E♯
D♯m7
6fr
C♯7(sus4)
4fr
B
F♯
A♯m7/E♯
D.S. al Coda
Coda
F♯
A♯m7
D♯m7
6fr
C♯7(sus4)
4fr
I think I see you.
B
F♯
N.C.

D♯m7
6fr
C♯7(sus4)
4fr
B
F♯
A♯m7/E♯
D♯m7
6fr
C♯7(sus4)
4fr
B
F♯
A♯m7/E♯
Bmaj7
C♯
4fr
D♯m
6fr
F♯

Bmaj7
C♯
D♯m
'Cause you're a sky, you're a sky full of stars.
F♯
Bmaj7
C♯
Such a heav-en-ly view.
D♯m
F♯
Bmaj7
You're such a heav-en-ly view.

C♯
4fr
D♯m
6fr
F♯
Bmaj7
C♯7(sus4)
4fr
D♯m
6fr
F♯m
Bmaj7
C♯7(sus4)
4fr
D♯m
6fr
D♯m7
6fr
(Ooh.
8vb
Bmaj7
C♯7(sus4)
4fr
D♯m
6fr
N.C.
Ooh.)
8vb

Say Something

Words & Music by Mike Campbell, Chad Vaccarino
& Ian Axel

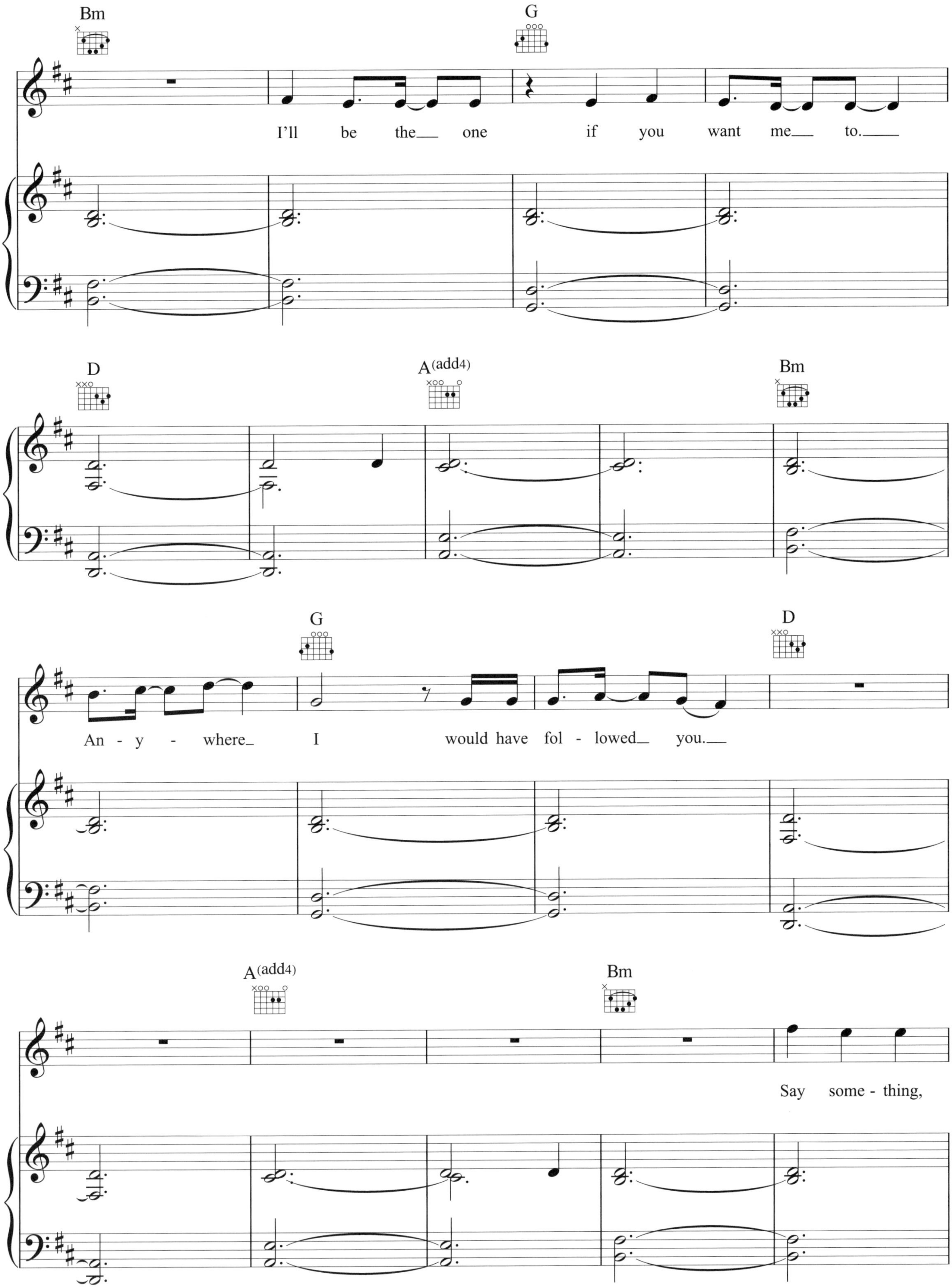
Bm
G
I'll be the one if you want me to.
D
A(add4)
Bm
G
D
Any - where I would have fol - lowed you.
A(add4)
Bm
Say some - thing,

G
D
I'm giv - ing up on you.
A(add4)
D
And I
F♯m(♭6)
am feel - ing so small.
Gsus2
It was o - ver my head;

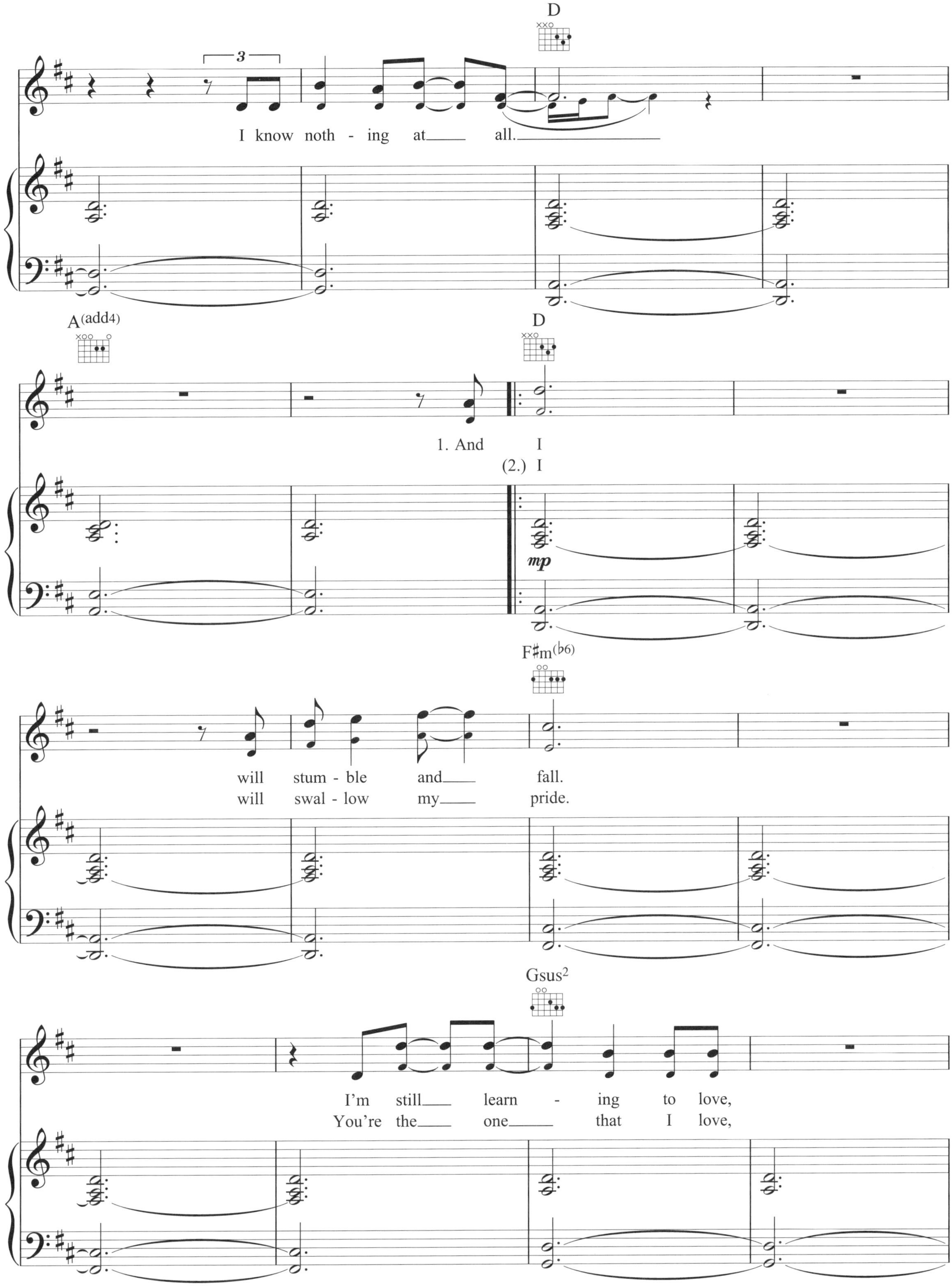
D
I know noth - ing at all.
A(add4)
D
1. And I
(2.) I
mp
F♯m(♭6)
will stum - ble and fall.
will swal - low my pride.
Gsus2
I'm still learn - ing to love,
You're the one that I love,

D
just start - ing to crawl.
and I'm say - ing good - bye.
A(add4)
Bm
Say some - thing,
Say some - thing,
cresc.
mf-f
8vb
G
D5
A(add4)
I'm giv - ing up on you.
I'm giv - ing up on you.
Bm
G
I'm sor - ry that I could - n't get
And I'm sor - ry that I could - n't get

D5
A(add4)
to you.
to you.
Bm
G
Any - where
And any - where
I would have fol - lowed you.
D5/A
2fr
A(add4)
Bm
G
1.
D
Say some - thing, I'm giv - ing up on you.

2.
A(add4)
D5
2. And
A(add4)
Bm
G
Say some - thing, I'm giv - ing
p sub.
D
A(add4)
up on you.
rit.
Bm
G
D
Say some - thing.
8vb

Somewhere Only We Know

Words & Music by Richard Hughes, Tim Rice-Oxley
& Tom Chaplin

Cm
3fr
F(sus4)
F
I knew the path - way like the back of my hand.
I felt the branch - es of it look - ing at me.
B♭
Dm/A
I felt the earth be - neath my feet.
Is this the place we used to love?
Cm
3fr
F(sus4)
F
Sat by the riv - er and it made me com - plete.
Is this the place that I've been dream - ing of?

Gm
Dm
Oh, sim - ple thing, where have you gone?
Oh, sim - ple thing, where have you gone?
Eb
1.
Cm rit.
F(sus4)
F
I'm get - ting tired and I need some - one to re - ly on.
I'm get - ting old and I need
2.
Cm
F(sus4)
F6
Cm
some - thing to re - ly on.
And if you have a
Con pedale

B♭/D
Cm
3fr
min - ute, why don't we go talk a - bout it
B♭/D
Cm
3fr
some - where on - ly we know. This could be the
B♭/D
To Coda
E♭maj7
6fr
F6
rit.
end of ev - 'ry - thing. So why don't we go. some - where on - ly we

E6
B♭/F
F6
F(sus2)
B♭
know.
Some-where on-ly we know.
a tempo ♩ = 84
Gm
3fr
Dm
Fm
(Ah,
ah.
Ah,
Cm
3fr
Am
Em
ah.
Ah,
ah.

B♭
D
Ah,
ah.)
Gm
Dm
Oh, sim - ple thing,
where have you gone?
E♭
Cm
rit.
F(sus4)
D7/F♯
I'm get - ting old and I need some - one to re - ly on.
a tempo ♩ = 84
Gm
Dm
So tell me when
you're gon - na let me in.

D.S. al Coda
E♭
Cm
F7(sus4)
F6
I'm get - ting tired and I need some-where to be - gin.
Coda
a tempo ♩ = 80
E♭maj7
rit.
F6
D7/F♯
Gm7
So why don't we go some-where on - ly we know.
rit.
Slower
Gm
E♭maj7
F6/9
Dm7/E♭
B♭
Some-where on - ly we know.

Speechless

Words & Music by Stefani Germanotta

F
G
hands up, ba - by you gave up, you gave up. I
heart seams, all my bub - ble dreams, bub - ble dreams. I
Am
G
can't be - lieve how you looked at me with your James Dean glos - sy eyes. In your
can't be - lieve how you looked at me with your John - ny Walk - er eyes. He's gon - na
F
G
N.C.
tight jeans with your long hair and your cig - ar - ette stained lies.
get you and aft - er he's through there's gon' be no love left to rye.
Am
E7/G♯
C/G
Could we fix you if you broke and is your punch
And I know that it's com - pli - ca - ted, but I'm a los - er in love. So ba - by, raise a glass to mend all the

F♯7♭5 C G/B Am G
4fr
line just a joke? I'll never talk again. Oh, boy you've left me
broken hearts of all my wrecked up friends.
F Gsus4 G
speechless, you've left me speechless, so speechless.
C G/B Am G Fmaj7 F6
And I'll never love again. Oh, boy you've left me speechless, you've left me
2° friend
1. 2.
Gsus4 G N.C. Gsus4 G
speechless, so speechless. 2. Oh, I speechless, so speechless. Oh.

C
G/B
Am
G
F
Oh.
Oh.
1.
2.
G
G
F
Oh.
And af - ter all the drinks and
E7
C
G/B
Am
bars that we've been to
would you give it all up? Could I give it all up for
you?
F
E7
And af - ter all the boys and the girls that we've been through
would you

rit.
C G/B B♭ F
give it all up? Could you give it all up? If I prom-ise boy,__ to you...
a tempo
C G/B Am F C G/B
That I'll nev-er talk a-gain. And I'll nev-er love a-
Am F C G/B Am G
-gain. I'll nev-er write a song, won't e-ven sing a-
F9 Gsus4 N.C. C G/B Am
-long. I'll nev-er love a-gain. Oh.__ So speech-less.__

Fmaj7 F6 Gsus4 G
You left me speech-less, so speech-less.
C G/B Am Fmaj7 F6
Will you ev-er talk a-gain? Oh, boy, why you so speech-less? You've left me
Gsus4 G C G/B
speech-less, so speech-less. Some men may fol-low
Am G F9 N.C. C
me but you choose "death and com-pan-y." Why you so speech-less? Oh, oh.
8vb

Stay With Me

Words & Music by Sam Smith, James Napier & William Phillips

Am7
F
C
These nights never seem to go to plan.
And deep down I know this never works.
Am7
F6
C
I don't want you to leave, will you hold my hand?
But you can lay with me so it does-n't hurt.
Oh, won't you
Am
F
C
stay with me?
'Cause you're
Am
F
C
all I need.

To Coda
Em/G Am F C E7/G♯
This ain't love, it's clear to see. But darl - ing
Am F C
1. 2.
Am F C
stay with me. Oh, oh.
Am F C C/G
1. 2.
Oh, oh. Oh, Oh, won't you

Am F C Am F C G5 3fr
stay with me? 'Cause you're all I need. This ain't
Am F C E7/G♯ Am F C
love, it's clear to see. But darl - ing stay with me.
Coda
D.S. al Coda
Am F C
Oh, won't you stay with me.

A Thousand Years

Words & Music by David Hodges & Christina Perri

B♭/D
Gm
F/A
stand a - lone, all of my doubt_ sud-den-ly goes a-way some -
front of me. Ev-er-y breath,_ ev-er-y hour has come to
Cm7
Gm
F
- how.
this.
One step clo - ser…
B♭
F/A
Gm7
F
I have died ev'ry day wait - ing for you. Darl-ing don't be a-fraid I have loved_ you for a

1.
2.
E♭
Fsus4
F
E♭maj7
B♭
F/A
Gm7
6fr
3fr
8vb
thou - sand years. I'll love you for a thou - sand more.
thou - sand more. And
all a-long I be-lieved I would find you. Time has brought your heart to me. I have loved_ you for a

E♭
Fsus4
F
thou - sand years. I'll love you for a thou - sand more.
8vb
B♭
F/A
Gm
F
E♭
Fsus4
F
Cm7
Gm
F
One step clo - ser,

Cm
3fr
F
Gm7
3fr
F
one step clo - ser…
B♭
F/A
Gm7
3fr
F
I have died ev - 'ry day wait - ing for you. Darl - ing don't be a - fraid, I have loved you for a
E♭
6fr
Fsus4
F
thou - sand years. I'll love you for a thou - sand more. And

B♭ F/A Gm7 F
all a long I be-lieved I would find you. Time has brought your heart to me. I have loved_ you for a
E♭ Fsus4 F
thou - sand years. I'll love you for a thou - sand more.
8vb
E♭ B♭/D
E♭ Gm rit. F E♭add9

Turning Tables

Words & Music by Ryan Tedder & Adele Adkins

Fm9
A♭
4fr
— have is on the floor.
— Where love is lost your ghost was found.
Cm7
3fr
A♭maj9
3fr
God on - ly knows what we're fight - ing for. All that I
I braved a hun - dred storms to leave you. As hard as you try,
Fm9
A♭
4fr
3
— say, you al-ways say more.
— no I will nev - er be knocked down.
A♭
4fr
Fm7
I can't keep up with your turn - ing ta - bles. Un - der

A♭
A♭sus2
B♭
your thumb I can't breath. So
Cm7
A♭maj7
E♭
I won't let you close enough to hurt
Fm
Cm7
A♭maj7
me. No, I won't res - cue
E♭
Fm
Cm7
A♭maj9
you to just de - sert me. I can't give you the

A♭ E♭/G Gm/B♭ B♭ Fm7 E♭ A♭add9
heart you think you gave me. It's time to say good - bye.
Cm7
To turn - ing ta - bles.
A♭maj9 Fm9
To turn - ing ta - bles.
A♭
To Coda

Cm7
3fr
A♭maj7
4fr
Next time I'll be brav - er, I'll be my
E♭
6fr
own sav - iour when the thun - der calls for me.
Fm7
Cm7
3fr
Next time I'll be brav - er,
A♭maj7
4fr
E♭
6fr
I'll be my own sav - iour, stand - ing

B♭
D.S. al Coda
N.C.
on my own two feet.
Coda
A♭
4fr
Cm7
3fr
3
Turn - ing ta - bles.
Vocal ad lib.
A♭maj9
3fr
Fm9
A♭maj9
3fr
Cm
3fr

1 2 3 4 5 6 7 8 9

HOW TO DOWNLOAD YOUR MUSIC TRACKS

1. Carefully remove your Download Card from the inside back cover of this book.

2. On the back of the card is your unique access code. Enter this at www.musicsalesdownloads.com

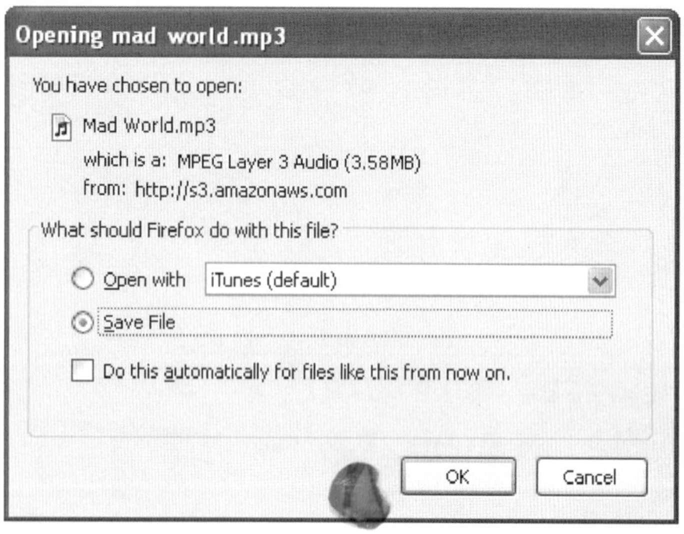

3. Follow the instructions to save your files to your computer*. That's it!

*Appearance of download manager will vary depending upon operating system and web browser.
In case of difficulty when downloading files, please contact dropcards.com/help
Card missing? Please contact music@musicsales.co.uk